D1490800

CERTAINTY

Is Science All You Need?

TROY VAN VOORHIS

ISBN: 0615988725
ISBN-13: 978-0615988726

ABOUT THIS SERIES

VeriTalks were created to cultivate ongoing conversations seeded by live Veritas Forum events.

Each VeriTalk includes both the original talk and audience Q&A to draw you more intimately into the conversation. Discussion questions—both personal and intellectual—are incorporated into the talk to deepen your engagement with the material, ideally in the company of friends. The questions are repeated at the end of the book for easy reference.

We hope this series will catalyze your exploration of True Life.

CONTENTS

ACKNOWLEDGMENTS

This talk was originally presented at The Veritas Forum at the California Institute of Technology in 2013 under the title, "Is Science Enough?"

Many thanks to the students, faculty and campus organizations who helped create this event.

This publication was made possible through the support of a grant from the John Templeton Foundation. The opinions expressed in this publication are those of the author and do not necessarily reflect the views of the John Templeton Foundation.

CERTAINTY: IS SCIENCE ALL YOU NEED?

TONIGHT WE ARE GOING to discuss science and faith and whether science by itself is enough to lead to human certainty. Now, when people find out that I'm a chemist and also a Christian I often get puzzled looks: "Doesn't that cause a lot of problems for you?" To which my honest answer is, "No. Not really. Why do you ask?"

And when I delve a little bit deeper, usually these questions arise out of some misconception that the asker has about science or faith. Either misperception on the one hand about what science does or does not offer us, or misconception on the other hand about what faith requires of the believer.

So to start off with, I want to summarize several of these misconceptions to get them out of the way so they don't color the entire discussion. In particular, I think this process of dispelling myths will help us listen better to one another without continually circling back to these common misconceptions.

CERTAINTY

MISCONCEPTIONS ABOUT SCIENCE

Misconception #1: Good scientists become atheists. This is an argument that has been championed by folks such as Richard Dawkins and Daniel Dennet, the so-called "New Atheists," or as I like to call them, the "Evangelical Atheists." The idea seems to be that in becoming a scientist, the repeated application of objective observation will somehow cure you of your misguided notions of faith. Thus, if you're a good scientist, you'll eventually become an atheist.

Now, like all the misconceptions we're going to discuss tonight, there's a kernel of truth here. And the kernel of truth is that to be a good scientists you *do* have to be able to make objective observations. If I do an experiment and collect data and then analyze that data in a biased way – for example by deleting the data points that don't agree with the conclusion I want to draw – the end result is not simply *bad* science, it is *not* science.

Let me give you another example. If I ran a chemical reaction and I found that I got 125% yield, I might respond by saying, "God suspended the law of conservation of mass in the middle of organic chemistry lab just for me. I deserve an A++ for this." And in that case my bias, namely my desire to get a good grade in O-Chem, would have caused me to reject a plausible hypothesis – namely, that I had mis-measured the amount of starting material for the reaction – in favor of a less plausible one. Doing science requires me to report and analyze my data in an objective, unbiased manner.

The argument then goes that, clearly, not believing in God is more objective than believing in Him, so all good scientists must be atheists. QED. But this argument has gone off the rails because atheism is every bit as biased a position as theism is.

Science can no more prove the non-existence of God than it can prove the existence of God.

It would seem then that we are stuck. We have two positions here, atheism and theism, and they're both biased. What do we do?

Well, we shouldn't really be surprised by this because scientists have all kinds of biases: intellectual, social, emotional biases. We bring all kinds of baggage into the lab with us. And the secret to being a good scientist isn't that you have to become some kind of unfeeling, cold, unbiased robot that just performs experiments. The secret to being a good scientist is to recognize your biases and leave them outside the lab when you come in so that you can perform objective testing. And in this respect, atheism doesn't provide any particular advantage or disadvantage. It's just another bias you need to check at the door.

Misconception #2: Science is making God irrelevant. Here, the argument goes something like this: In ancient times we needed God to explain all kinds of things we didn't understand - like thunder, drought and disease. However, now science teaches us how all of these things happen in terms of chemistry, physics and biology. And so we find ourselves needing God less and less and eventually we won't need Him at all. This understanding of science and faith is often known as the "God of the gaps" picture of the relationship between science and faith, and it is also flawed.

The key fallacy at work here is that God can only exist in those phenomena that science cannot explain, that the expansion of science necessarily squeezes God into smaller and smaller boxes. But the truth is that God is not just the God of the gaps, but the God of everything. The truth is that as science gets bigger, God gets bigger. Or at least our understanding of him does. Because Christians believe that God exists not just in the things science can't explain but also in the things that it can.

For example, I could tell you that the North Star is actually a collection of five astronomical bodies that are 434 light years away from planet earth. But those facts don't detract from the majesty of a God who created those astronomical bodies and set them into orbit. Rather, the evidence adds to my awe and wonder.

And so it's not true that science is making God irrelevant. To some extent, science makes God even more relevant.

Misconception #3: Science is *the* path to certainty. This misconception is going to be important for what we discuss later, so I'm going to dwell on it for a bit longer. On some level, it is natural to think that scientific inquiry is the only way to be really certain. After all, science is based on evidence – things we can examine and measure – and, as they say, seeing is believing. People who hold this view often characterize faith as some kind of flimsy guesswork – something that can't really lead to certainty at all.

Now, of course scientific evidence can increase our confidence in a proposition. But confidence is not the same as certainty. As the saying goes, you can tell a person there are 300 sextillion stars in the universe and he will believe you. But tell that same person that a bench is covered in wet paint and he will need to touch it to be sure. Because there is a difference between confidence and certainty.

Only in pure mathematics is reason alone enough to produce absolute certainty. In the natural world, things rarely work out so neatly. If I have a hypothesis, there's typically going to be evidence that supports the hypothesis and evidence that goes against the hypothesis. As Richard Feynman once said, in science, "We have found it of paramount importance that in order to progress we must recognize … ignorance and leave room for doubt. Scientific knowledge is a body of statements of varying degrees of certainty – some most unsure, some nearly sure, none absolutely certain." Even for a theory with no known exceptions, in science one must always be wary – because there's always the chance that when more data comes in, the model will turn out to be wrong. And classical mechanics will give way to quantum mechanics. Newton will be followed by Einstein.

The reality is that science has made great contributions to human knowledge, but not any significant contributions to human certainty.

CERTAINTY

QUESTIONS FOR DISCUSSION

The secret to being a good scientist is to recognize your bias and leave it at the door so you can do objective testing. To what extent have you found this possible? Have you found certain biases to be limiting for you? How did you leave them at the door?

Can you think of situations in which science makes God more – rather than less – relevant?

What is the difference between confidence and certainty?

? For an audience question related to this topic, see page 26 (*Hasn't science proven there is no truth?*).

MISPERCEPTIONS ABOUT FAITH

Misperception #1: Having faith means you can't believe in
_____. I've left a blank there so you can fill it in with your favorite controversial scientific idea: evolution, the Big Bang, dinosaurs, etc. And this is a really big one, so I want to get it on the table first. There's a real fear that in becoming a Christian or a Muslim or a Jew you must accept not only God, but a whole host of other positions that run counter to scientific evidence.

Once again, there's a kernel of truth here. And the kernel of truth is that there are, historically speaking, any number of questions on which science and the Church have been at odds. How old is the universe? What are the origins of species? Does the earth revolve around the sun or the sun revolve around the earth?

On the Christian side, most of these arguments are based on Biblical scriptures. As a Christian, I believe the Bible is true and free from error. And the Bible does provide a great deal of evidence about God's work in the natural world. But just as scientific evidence requires interpretation to have meaning, so too does scriptural evidence require interpretation to have meaning.

For example, take the issue of spontaneous generation – the idea that inanimate objects under the right conditions can spontaneously bring forth life. Think, for example, of maggots forming in a bowl of corn meal. For about two thousand years, the dominant scientific interpretation of this fact was that corn meal and air came together to spontaneously *make* maggots. On the Christian side, early scholars looked at passages like quail appearing to the Israelites in the dessert or Sampson discovering a beehive growing in the carcass of a lion and they concluded that the Bible also supports spontaneous generation. Everyone agreed!

But then, in the latter part of the 19th century, Louis Pasteur clearly showed that spontaneous generation is not the normal course of things. And the conclusion from this isn't that the old experiments and scripture are wrong. The old experiments had not been falsified – maggots really do form in corn meal (If you don't believe me, go home and try it). And Christians continue to believe that the Israelites did find quail in the dessert. The experiments and the scripture were not wrong. They had just been *misinterpreted*. Life does not come out of non-life as a matter of course. When that happens, something unusual, even miraculous, has occurred. Thus we see that scripture requires interpretation.

We have been given the scriptures, the ability to reason and the opportunity to pray for guidance. Christians believe that by judicious application of these tools, we can arrive at Truth. I can understand how people think that me becoming a Christian means I accepted without question some universal doctrine of what scripture teaches about science. But the reality is that my walk as a Christian is more one of using scripture and prayer and, yes, reason to seek the Truth. So being a Christian does not necessarily mean you can't believe in whatever your favorite controversial topic is.

Misperception #2: Faith means ignoring evidence. Here, the idea is that faith means believing things in spite of incontrovertible evidence to the contrary. People of faith are the kind of people who believe the Apollo moon landing was fake, while professional wrestling is real. Faith means when you're confronted with evidence you don't like you just ignore it or attempt to explain it away.

This description is characteristic of *blind* faith. We meet people who have blind faith all the time. But this is not the kind of faith that God requires or even desires. As Thomas Merton said: "Faith is a decision. It is a judgment that is fully and deliberately taken in light of a truth that cannot be proven. It is not merely the acceptance of a decision that has been made by somebody else."

Faith does not give us an excuse to ignore evidence. Christians believe that God left evidence of his actions here on earth and he expects us to examine that evidence. Indeed, much of the Bible is written for this very purpose. For that reason the writer of the Gospel of Luke introduces his gospel: "It seemed good to me, having followed all things closely for some time, to write an orderly account for you that you may have *certainty* concerning the things you have been taught."

There is all manner of historical evidence for Christianity: the empty tomb, the consistency of the early Christians' testimony, their perseverance under duress. It is not incontrovertible, but the evidence is there if you want to look for it.

CERTAINTY

QUESTIONS FOR DISCUSSION

How would you fill in the blank: Faith means you have to accept not only God, but _____, which runs counter to scientific evidence. How do Professor Van Voorhis' comments square with those fears?

Professor Van Voorhis says that he uses prayer, scripture and reason to seek after the truth in controversial areas. Whatever your faith background, what resources do you find most helpful in seeking after truth? Are there limits to these resources; and how do you use them judiciously?

Re-read the passage by Thomas Merton. How do you respond to the idea that there is "a truth that cannot be proven"?

Professor Van Voorhis briefly mentions some historical evidence for Christianity: the empty tomb, the consistency of the early Christians' testimony, their perseverance under duress. What do you know about these pieces of evidence? Do you find them compelling?

? For audience questions related to this topic, see page 25 (*How do you explain the evil things done in the name of Christianity?*), page 27 (*How do you reconcile evolution with your Christian faith?*), page 30 (*If the core laws of the physical world are simple, why are the theological arguments of Christianity so chaotic?*) and page 34 (*Can you share an example of evidence that's shaken your faith?*).

INTEGRATING SCIENCE AND FAITH

For these reasons and a variety of other reasons, I believe the popular caricature of science and faith as being mutually exclusive is just that: a caricature. So let's get to the main event: the integration of science and faith. How can science and faith be integrated? How do they work together? How can they work together? How should they work together?

To organize our discussion of this admittedly broad point, I want to draw your attention to the visual aid below, which summarizes the three subjects I most want to know about in this life: I want to learn about the universe, about God (or Gods) should they exist and I want to learn about me. And I should note that this figure is not drawn to scale.

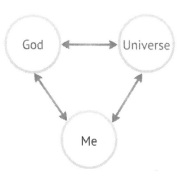

Science and faith work together to help us understand what knowledge in these spheres looks like and how they interact with each other. So we will frame our discussion with three questions we want to answer: What is **God** like if He or She exists? How does the **universe** work? And what about **me**? How do I fit into all of this?

Question #1: What is God like? Obviously faith has a number of things to say about this question. One could even argue that's the whole point of faith: to figure out what God is like.

But for those who believe that God played a role in the construction of the universe we live in, natural science also offers a tremendous opportunity to learn about God. Because natural science is the study of God's handiwork. I would even go so far as to say that if you are a natural scientist and also a Christian, you are hard pressed not to feel a sense of wonder at the world he has created. Isaac Newton said: "It is the perfection of God's works that they are all done with the greatest simplicity. He is the God of order and not of confusion."

Because while most would say that God is beyond comprehension, the universe offers a useful lower bound on the size and complexity of God: he has to be at least as big and grand as the universe he created.

When I look at how things organize on different levels: from the subatomic weirdness of quantum mechanics, to the way that atoms come together to form sophisticated molecules, to the way those molecules come together to form life that inhabits a vast galaxy that is in and of itself only one of millions and millions of galaxies in the universe … I begin to get a little bit of a glimpse of what God must be like and how he works.

Because we are humans, we're going to understand God best on our length scale – his concern for people and how they behave – but God is not just a God of people but of quarks and quasars, too. Science and faith both have things to teach us about God.

Question #2: How does the universe work? This is kind of a gimme for science. Of *course* science helps us understand how the universe works. What's not as clear is what role faith plays in this. Some would even argue this is a question that faith ought to keep away from; at best, faith provides simplistic and incorrect models that are going to be embarrassingly disproved by later scientific testing. But this argument assumes there can only be one explanation and ignores the existence of multiple layers of meaning.

Let me give you an example. You could ask me, "Troy, why is your shirt purple?" I could answer this in a scientific way: "My shirt is purple because there is a high concentration of $6,6'$-dibromoindigo in the fibers that were used to weave it." I could even test that hypothesis by attempting to remove the dye from the shirt, to demonstrate the molecular reason why my shirt is purple.

However, I could offer another explanation: "My shirt is purple because my wife thinks I look quite nice in purple." Two different explanations for the same phenomenon. Both are correct, but neither is complete.

The explanations of science and faith coexist in precisely this way. For example, we could ask the question "Why do bacteria have flagella?" One explanation would be as follows: "Bacteria have flagella because of an evolutionary process. First, a secretory system arose, which later led to the development of a protoflagellum which finally evolved into the eubacterial flagellum we know today." Another explanation would be: "Bacteria have flagella because God wanted them to be able to swim." Coexisting explanations with different layers of meaning.

And this interaction of science and faith in explaining how the natural world works is far from trivial. Because in the scientific exercise, we always go in with the assumption that there is a *reason* why things are the way they are. We assume that the universe is going to make sense. But why should we expect it to turn out this way? As Einstein once said: "The most incomprehensible thing about the universe is that it is comprehensible."

And the Christian response to this conundrum is that there *is* an explanation: The universe was created by a rational, personal deity. And so we can expect that there will be a reason why things are the way they are. There's no observation such that when I ask "why?" the ultimate answer will be: "Why ask why? There's no reason. There's just random chance."

And for me this premise comes to its sharpest point in the field of quantum mechanics, one of the fields that I dearly love, because the laws of quantum mechanics tell us that there are certain experiments for which you cannot predict the outcome of the experiment until after you've done the experiment itself. You can predict the probability of a given outcome, but you can't tell me what the outcome is actually going to be. And so there are certain scientific questions you can ask me, like "Why did the neutron spin turn out to be up as opposed to down?" And there's no scientific reason. It's just random.

But the Christian response to this is to say that even this was not random. Even though we could not predict the outcome of the experiment in advance, ultimately there is a reason why it turned out the way it did, because there is nothing random in a world that is orchestrated by God.

So I think that science and faith both have things to teach us about how the world works, particularly in areas where their explanations overlap.

Question #3: How do I fit into all this? This is a question that science by itself is particularly ill-equipped to answer. The central problem is that science can never lead to any kind of truth that addresses me, the individual. The basis for scientific inquiry is the assumption that truth is objective – that is to say that truth is an *object* that exists independent of the observation by the *subject*, namely, me. Thus, by definition, science divorces truth from the truth-seeker.

In one of the most wonderful passages of scripture, Jesus taught his disciples "You shall know the Truth and the Truth will set you free." By contrast, the promise of science is the somewhat more mundane, "You shall know the truth, but the truth will probably not have any perceptible impact on the way you chose to behave." Because scientific Truth is out there, and I am over here.

This problem is one that all of academia faces. Let's say you took an ethics class in moral rationalism (the idea that right and wrong can be deduced based on rational arguments alone). You read philosophers like Plato and Kant and Richard Hare and in class you demonstrate how injunctions like "it is wrong to lie" and "it is unjust not to share with those in need" follow from rational arguments alone. Now, consider two possible final examinations in that class. The first asks you to write an essay using the principles of moral rationalism to prove the statement, "Truth telling is always right." I suspect some of you have taken just such an examination.

The second exam also consists of just one question: "In class, we used moral rationalism to show that lying and not sharing with the needy are wrong. During the course of this semester, how many times did you lie or fail to share what you have with those in need? Grading will be as follows: minus one point for every lie, minus five points for every failure to share. And minus 100 points for lying in response to this question."

We can laugh at this because we don't expect the things we learn in class to impact the way that we behave. The truth is out there and we are over here. And to me this is one of the weaknesses of a purely scientific worldview: it possesses no power to change people. And this is the place where faith becomes crucial in science, turning it from a cold exercise into something that can be vibrant and life-giving.

CERTAINTY

QUESTIONS FOR DISCUSSION

People of faith often focus on how God interacts with humans. But what could God's interaction with the natural world tell us? In other words, what are the implications if God is the God of quarks? The God of quasars?

How might viewing the world as having multiple layers of meaning change your experience of suffering or injustice? How might you differently interpret joy or satisfaction?

What conclusions do you reach upon reflecting on Einstein's words: "The only incomprehensible thing about the universe is that it's comprehensible"?

"We don't expect the things we learn in class to impact the way that we behave." Why is this? Have you experienced times classroom learning did translate into changed behavior? What might it look like for this to be the norm?

? For an audience question related to this topic, see page 29 *(Should science have a role in determining morality?).*

CONFIDENCE, CERTAINTY AND CHANGE

To understand why we need faith to accomplish this transformation, we must realize it is our convictions – the things that we are absolutely certain of – that govern the way that we behave.

If I am going to organize my life around a principle, I want to be absolutely certain that that principle is true. If I am uncertain, I'll be inclined to wait for all the evidence to come in before I act. But this doesn't work, because from a scientific perspective, there is *always* more evidence we could gather. Scientific evidence can give us greater and greater confidence, but it never gets us all the way across the gap from indecision to certainty. It might leave a big gap, or a small gap. But there is always a gap. The last step is always a step of faith.

Now this need not be *religious* faith – we can have faith in the goodness of humanity, faith in a person, or even faith in the law of gravity – but making decisions requires faith. Because faith is the thing that gives us a framework for making decisions in the light of incomplete evidence.

Confidence. Let me give you an example. Suppose I feel there is convincing evidence that human activity is contributing significantly to global climate change. This is a hypothetical; I'm not trying to make the case one way or the other. But suppose I am convinced. But despite being convinced, I still drive an SUV; I still leave incandescent lightbulbs on in my house when I'm not home; I still fly tens of thousands of miles for my vacations every year.

In this instance I would contend that while I am convinced, I am not certain. Because if I was certain, I would change the way I behave. The fact that I persist in doing things that produce large amounts of CO_2 is evidence that proves one of two things: either I am *not* sure that what I'm doing is contributing to global warming or that I *am* sure and I'm a fundamentally evil person who does not care about the future of our planet or the security of our country or the well-being of my own children.

Certainty. Thus, what I need is the kind of certainty that is capable of changing how I behave. Because I am not perfect. And neither are any of my scientific or religious colleagues. In my mind, this is the primary argument for the Christian faith over and above any other framework of faith because the Christian faith provides not only a framework for making decisions but the *means* to act according to those decisions.

And the means is the person of Jesus Christ, because Christians believe that when I place my faith in Jesus, then the person of Christ comes to live in me. And what I fundamentally believe is Jesus' ability to change me, to change who I am, to make my life different.

Let me explain why that is so important to me. In high school I was a geek. I know that comes as a shock to many of you: a quantum mechanics professor at MIT and you were a geek in high school? Shocking but true. I was too smart for my own good, I was socially awkward, I was unathletic, and to boot, I grew too quickly so that six months out of every year my clothes would be too small for me. And the unfortunate truth is that chicks don't dig tall, awkward, scrawny dudes who don't know how to dress themselves.

And so in the social structure of my high school, there were the popular kids and then there were kids like me. And I was one of the unpopular kids who desperately wanted to be cool. And it didn't make me a very nice person. I shunned people who I thought were lower on the social ladder than I was – the other people who didn't have the money to wear the right kind of clothes, or the other members of the Chemistry Olympiad team, who (in my opinion) were far nerdier than me.

Life outside of high school didn't really turn out all that different for me. As time went on, I found myself simply replacing "popularity" with any of a host of other ultimate goals: good grades, success in my career, wealth, fame. Because the problem isn't with high school. Or the "in" crowd. Or college. Or academia. The problem is *me*. The way that I am. The things that I want. No matter how hard I work, it's never a problem I can solve because I *am* the problem..

And theistic naturalism doesn't provide me any help here, because if God merely set the universe in motion and then hung up a sign saying: "Be back in 25 million years" then I'm stuck. Whatever I am is whatever I am.

And in fact most religions are even less help on this point because they tie acceptance by God with our performance: our ability to live by a certain set of rules or to accomplish a handful of tasks.

Change. Only in Christianity does God provide the means for us to change who we are. The same God who set the universe in motion, who gives breath and life to every living thing, that same God sent to us the means of our redemption in Jesus Christ, because in Christianity you don't do good as a way to suck up to God and convince Him that you're better than all the non-Christians. Morality in Christianity isn't a ladder that we have to ascend to get close to God. The entire narrative of Christianity isn't a story of people raising themselves up to God. Christianity is the story of *God who came down* to us. The same God who set the universe in motion, who gives breath and life to every living thing ... that same God sent to us the means of our redemption. And for me, this theistic Christian worldview provides the most satisfying answer to the question, "What about me? Where do I fit into the universe?" I am looking forward to our discussion of these questions.

QUESTIONS FOR DISCUSSION

What principles do you organize your life around? Can you identify 2-3 absolute convictions that govern the way you behave?

Do you ever experience a disconnect between the way you want to live and the ability to carry out your intentions? Where do you find the means to act according to your convictions or how do you deal with your inability to do so?

Professor Van Voorhis contrasts faith systems where one must prove or earn God's acceptance with Christianity, where God's acceptance is a gift that cannot be earned. What are the implications of these different systems for the way one chooses to live? What do you think about the possibility of Jesus Christ as the means of transformation in one's life?

What about you: where do you fit? Suppose the Christian God really exists: how does that change your place in the universe?

? For audience questions related to this topic, see page 31 *(Can certainty be detrimental?)*, page 33 *(Why couldn't a person take responsibility to change their own behavior? Why rely on Jesus to change you?)* and page 36 *(It sounds like you're deciding truth based on what's useful or gives you purpose. Is that true?).*

QUESTION AND ANSWER

CERTAINTY

Summary of Questions from the Audience

- How do you explain the evil things done in the name of Christianity? (Answer on page 25)

- Hasn't science proven there is no truth? (Answer on page 26)

- How do you reconcile evolution with your Christian faith? (Answer on page 27)

- Should science have a role in determining morality? (Answer on page 29)

- If the core laws of the physical world are simple, why are the theological arguments of Christianity so chaotic? (Answer on page 30)

- Do you think certainty can be detrimental? (Answer on page 31)

- Why couldn't a person take responsibility to change their own behavior? Why rely on Jesus to change you? (Answer on page 33)

- Can you share an example of evidence that's shaken your faith? (Answer on page 34)

- It sounds like you're deciding truth based on what's useful or gives you purpose. Is that true? (Answer on page 36)

Question and Answer Session

Audience member: You've pointed out many positive things about Christianity, but when we look at history we see how dark it is. With the same name, so many horrible things have happened. How do you explain that?

Van Voorhis: Certainly there are bad things that the Church has done in the history of the world. Unquestionably. There are also a lot of good things. Whether there are, on balance, more bad things that good things: who knows? I would never make the case that Christians are perfect or the paragons of virtue or have never done anything wrong: that would be false on the face of it.

The main role of the Church is not to be an example of what perfection looks like, but an example of what *being perfected* looks like. Perfection is a state. Being perfected is a process. And it can be a messy process. One where you fall on your face and recognize your errors and ask God to help you do better next time. And so yes, the Church has done bad things. That is part of what happens when imperfect people try to follow a perfect God.

Audience member: Many scientists are critical of religion. Why would I make the assumption of God? Like Laplace said during the reign of Napoleon, "I have no need of that hypothesis."

Van Voorhis: As for the Laplace point – "I have no need of this hypothesis, the hypothesis of God" – that works in so far as the only thing you want is a one-dimensional definition of truth which is a mechanistic version of truth: this causes this causes this. If I change this, this changes this changes this.

Audience member: No, I'm saying the assumption of truth. Why should there be a truth? Science has proven there is no truth. We are always proving ourselves wrong.

Van Voorhis: I would say science doesn't say there is no truth. I would give a much more positive spin on the interaction of science and truth. Science has done a very great thing: every scientist I know has a view that science is objective. This is the scientific point of view.

Whether or not they've thought deeply about it, scientists *live* as though there is an objective truth. We believe that we do the experiments and that it's pursing an objective truth that can be found; it's not some relative truth that's going to apply only to me personally. Whether or not that's integral to science, whether you could do science thinking there is no objective truth: perhaps you could. But procedurally I would say most scientists do believe there is objective truth.

Audience member: How do you reconcile evolution with your Christian faith?

Van Voorhis: I'll say from the outset, some of you are going to be disappointed because I'm not going to advocate for any of the political camps in the creation/evolution/intelligent design debate.

There are a huge range of different points of view, even amongst believing Christians in terms of how creation, evolution and intelligent design fit together. All the way from folks who believe the Bible is literally true and the world is 6,000 years old to people who believe that everything science has to say is true so any Biblical passage that has to do with the natural world should be interpreted figuratively. And there's everything in between.

The thing I want to encourage all of you to recognize is that both people who agree with you on this point and those who don't – and I find there are very few who don't have an opinion about this – that whether they share your view or not, these need to be based on honest grappling with scriptural evidence and scientific evidence and any other form of evidence you feel is appropriate in order to say, "This is why I think this is right." And to appreciate that in some cases it may be that people in the opposing camp also have evidence and may also have thought through their arguments and are not evil or stupid. Because I think that there is an objective truth on this.

The important first step toward uncovering this truth is to converse with each other in such a way that we are pursuing truth rather than me beating someone over the head until they agree with me. It is not worthwhile for me to say, "This is my opinion, come rally around me!" I think that actually sets the debate back, because right now I'm the only one who gets to talk. If it's going to be a fair debate it has to be two people or three or four, where you can actually hear each other out. And I encourage you to have those conversations together (or even with me after the Forum).

Audience member: Should science have any role in determining morality?

Van Voorhis: I think, yes. Because certainly there are times when we don't know the consequences of our actions until science says, actually what you're doing is this. And once we have the scientific evidence, I think we have every right to say, yes, this should impact our morality.

Now, you're going to say: "How much should this impact our morality?" There are certain things I don't think any scientific evidence is going to change, like: you shouldn't kill. There's no scientific evidence that's going to say, no you should kill, it's really good. So there are certain boundaries where there isn't any scientific evidence that's going to change a particular moral point.

But there are the finer details of things, like global warming, as an example, where scientific evidence would make an impact. If we found out human production of carbon dioxide doesn't influence global warming, that would impact our morality because there no longer would be a moral dimension to gas guzzling. Or if we find out that it really does, then there is a moral dimension to that. And then the evidence does impact our moral decisions.

Audience member: As a physicist, it seems like even though the world itself is incredibly complicated the core laws are actually incredibly simple. But studying the theological structure of Christianity, it seems like there are so many aspects, so many arguments and it's very chaotic. Why did Jesus come 2,000 years ago in this place, why are there angels, etc. So how do you speak to that?

Van Voorhis: I don't like reading theology either. But some of the difficulty there is one of culture: that in the social sciences argument and nuance are much, much more appreciated and desired than they are in physics. When I was in physics classes, I liked the simplicity of it. It really boils down to the Schrödinger equation, that's great.

So when you say you read theology and it doesn't appeal to you, I think it would probably be the same as if you read a sociology article or abstract economics article. I feel that same way: it's just not how I think about the world. It doesn't mean it's not true; doesn't mean all of sociology is false just because I don't like reading sociology articles.

It just means there's so much diversity among people that we can put the blinders on and say, "God only consists of that piece of God that I understand" or "The correct view of God is only the way I appreciate Him being." I don't think that can be true because there is such a diversity of people that for everybody to understand God in the same way we'd have to be uniform. We would have to like the same things and look at things the same way and that's not reality. So certainly when you look at some of these theological discussions, you just punt on it. I was having a conversation the other day about angels and demons and I had to say, "Dude, I really don't know much about their theology."

Audience member: Do you think certainty can be detrimental? Is it actually bad to believe in the absolute truth of something? I think that there are absolute truths, but I think that by accepting absolute truths we limit ourselves. So the real goal of science is to keep everything open, so there's always questioning, wondering whether or not we are incorrect. Is it possible by taking that last step of faith we are limiting ourselves?

Van Voorhis: I would agree with your first statement: certainty is dangerous. It is very dangerous. Because if you're certain about the wrong thing and you're really certain, you can cause a lot of damage. So I don't throw it around lightly and say everyone wants to be certain and then we'll be happy and get along. Certainty is a very dangerous thing.

Unfortunately, it's the least dangerous thing that we have. The opposite of certainty is inaction. So in my use of the word certainty, the Christian idea of certainty, is not the absence of doubt. I have doubts all the time about Christianity, but I'm certain of it, because I have the confidence and the certainty to act, as you said, as if it is true. That is certainty under the Christian definition of things.

There are lots of examples of people in the Bible having doubts. And it doesn't mean they didn't believe; they had doubts coexisting with belief. And the deciding factor according to Christianity is not, how many doubts did you have? Were you 99% certain? 98%? All the measures are based on decisions. The decision to act according to, or as if you believed something.

And there is a sense in Christianity that acting according to the belief reinforces your certainty of it. That certainty is an active process, not a passive process, not something you wait and wait and wait and then you receive certainty, but that it's tested through action. So when you say in science you have this idea that we're not 100% sure but we're going to go as if it is true but open to the possibility it might be wrong, I'd say that's still consistent with certainty in the way Christianity would define it. Does that make sense?

Audience member: An interesting side note from the philosophy of science is that's actually the end result of the philosophy of science: we can't be certain of anything, but by acting on something, we'll see if it came out to be true or not. I did this thing and what I expected to happen did and so with a certain higher degree of probability we can say it's true, but there's never 100% certainty.

Van Voorhis: And that aspect of science actually grew out of the fact that science was founded by a lot of people who were Christian, so they went in with this same kind of assumption about faith and truth. And they guessed that if they did this in science, it would also work — and it turned out that it did. And now people try to say you could have done this without Christianity. That's true. But that particular aspect of the Christian worldview was important for the development of science.

Audience member: Why couldn't a person take responsibility to change their own behavior? Why rely on Jesus to change you?

Van Voorhis: This is a very good question. I've certainly met atheists and agnostics who take this responsibility on themselves. It's certainly possible. You can say, "By the force of my own will, I'm going to pull myself up by my bootstraps and figure out how to live a moral life."

The problem, as I see it, is: What if you don't want to? What if you don't have quite enough energy? What if you're kind of tired that day, feel kind of lazy? There are all kinds of excuses we can throw up for why we don't do what is right. And to me this is a big problem, because there are a lot of times when I don't feel like doing it.

And in Christianity there's this whole process of transformation that's supernatural, that doesn't rely on my own strength, but relies on the strength of God. If we're going to have something that applies to everybody, that's universal, that doesn't just apply to those people who have really strong wills and really good self-control, but is going to apply to people with weak self-control and weak wills, it has to be something that offers them help, assistance in transforming into the person they really ought to be.

So my examples are not meant to imply that there can't be atheists who are moral, and it's not to imply that there's nothing that we can do to motivate ourselves to make good decisions. My point is that because of our limitations, there's always a limited degree to which I can make myself do what is right based on who I am and what I've got.

Audience member: You spoke of faith that could employ evidence. I'd like to hear of some examples of evidence that have shaken your faith.

Van Voorhis: So what's the one thing that shakes my faith, or makes me question my faith the most? I'll say: Is there life after death? Because Christianity certainly gives an answer to that: Yes, there is life after death and it's going to be great, according to what vague account there is in the Bible.

But that certainly seems almost too good to be true, doesn't it? If you're going to look at the physical world evidence, it seems like you die, you don't get up, that's it. When I was six I watched a special on National Geographic about how the sun was going to go supernova in about 5 billion years and I got really upset. Because I thought, "Even if I live that long, how am I going to survive that?" And it just hit me: I'm going to die someday. So I was kind of a morbid child.

So this sounds too good to be true. But what if there's nothing? So if I wake up at 3 a.m. and I'm anxious about something, it's likely to be that.

But the thing I always come back to is that as humans we have these notions of things like justice and rightness and hope for the future and the way things ought to be. And those are things that don't exist here in this world. They come from somewhere else.

And so when I think about it, I think: "There's got to be something more than this." I'm pretty confident of that. In my experience, I believe there's a God. Sometimes I question whether there's something after death, but I believe there's a God and I believe there's something more than this universe. That's based on my experience of God and my experience of life. And I think there's probably a way that human beings participate in that something more, because God is just. And so I end up saying: "Okay, fine. I find the proposition of heaven by itself very hard to believe, but I will believe in it because of other propositions related to faith that I do believe."

Which I think is important. I think sometimes people think Christians are Christians because of heaven. You know, that sounds really good, so I think I'll sign up. But for me, it's the opposite. I don't believe in God because I want to go to heaven; I want to go to heaven because I believe in God and I know what He's like, and apparently that's the end where we get to meet Him.

Audience member: It sounds like you're deciding truth based on what's useful or gives you purpose. Is that true?

Van Voorhis: I wouldn't necessarily disagree with that statement, but I'm not sure I would agree with it. If I was to say how I decide what's true about God, it's not like it's orthogonal to that or parallel to that, but they may be skew from each other or in different hyperplanes.

Because certainly I don't necessarily decide what I believe is true based on what is *useful* to me. The things I wrestle the most with are the things that will be useful to me because I keep getting confronted with them: Should I give money to the guy on the street? Should I say this to this person? Those are things that are useful to me so I wrestle with them a lot; there are other things that are not as useful to me, so I don't wrestle with them.

So utility definitely plays a role, but I wouldn't say it is decisive. Because deciding what is true based solely on utility is a very dangerous proposition. Because there are things that are useful and convenient that could be completely wrong. And so I would be nervous using that as my only metric for truth. I need something more than that.

In terms of purpose, I'm not sure of the cause and effect there. The things that are true about God do give me purpose. And I think there can be a way in which there is a feedback loop. Say I'm deciding between two truth propositions, and this truth proposition would lead to this purpose for my life and that one would lead to that purpose, then I can ask, which of those two seems more likely as the purpose for my life? That is *an* ingredient, but I wouldn't say it's the sole ingredient.

And there are certainly times where God's purpose for me has been a surprise to me. For example, to be honest, I didn't think God's plan for my life would be to be a professor at MIT. I had read some of those passages about how God doesn't like rich people or smart people and said, "Ah, God doesn't want me to be a professor at MIT!" But it turns out that's what He wanted, so that's where I went. So, yes, purpose also plays a role. But sometimes only in hindsight.

QUESTIONS FOR DISCUSSION

CERTAINTY

From *Misconceptions About Science* **(page 6)**

- The secret to being a good scientist is to recognize your bias and leave it at the door so you can do objective testing. To what extent have you found this possible? Have you found certain biases to be limiting for you? How did you leave them at the door?

- Can you think of situations in which science makes God more – rather than less – relevant?

- What is the difference between confidence and certainty?

From *Misperceptions About Faith* **(page 10)**

- How would you fill in the blank: Faith means you have to accept not only God, but _____, which runs counter to scientific evidence. How do Professor Van Voorhis' comments square with those fears?

- Professor Van Voorhis says that he uses prayer, scripture and reason to seek after the truth in controversial areas. Whatever your faith background, what resources do you find most helpful in seeking after truth? Are there limits to these resources; and how do you use them judiciously?

- Reread the passage by Thomas Merton. How do you respond to the idea that there is "a truth that cannot be proven"?

- Professor Van Voorhis briefly mentions some historical evidence for Christianity: the empty tomb, the consistency of the early Christians' testimony, their perseverance under duress. What do you know about these pieces of evidence? Do you find them compelling?

From *Integrating Science and Faith* **(page 16)**

- People of faith often focus on how God interacts with humans. But what could God's interaction with the natural world tell us? In other words, what are the implications if God is the God of quarks? The God of quasars?

- How might viewing the world as having multiple layers of meaning change your experience of suffering or injustice? How might you differently interpret joy or satisfaction?

- What conclusions do you reach upon reflecting on Einstein's words: "The only incomprehensible thing about the universe is that it's comprehensible"?

- "We don't expect the things we learn in class to impact the way that we behave." Why is this? Have you experienced times classroom learning did translate into changed behavior? What might it look like for this to be the norm?

From *Confidence, Certainty and Change* **(page 21)**

- What principles do you organize your life around? Can you identify 2-3 absolute convictions that govern the way you behave?

- Do you ever experience a disconnect between the way you want to live and the ability to carry out your intentions? Where do you find the means to act according to your convictions or how do you deal with your inability to do so?

- Professor Van Voorhis contrasts faith systems where one must prove or earn God's acceptance with Christianity, where God's acceptance is a gift that cannot be earned. What are the implications of these different systems for the way one chooses to live? What do you think about the possibility of Jesus Christ as the means of transformation in one's life?

• What about you: where do you fit? Suppose the Christian God really exists: how does that change your place in the universe?

ABOUT THE PRESENTER

Troy Van Voorhis is a professor of chemistry at MIT and an expert in electron transfer dynamics, solar energy, and molecular electronics. Van Voorhis received his bachelor's degree in chemistry and mathematics from Rice University and his PhD in chemistry from the University of California at Berkeley. Following a postdoctoral fellowship at Harvard, he joined the faculty of MIT.

His research focuses on the intersection of quantum mechanics and chemistry. In particular, his work addresses questions of how solar energy can be efficiently captured and stored. He is the author of numerous scholarly publications and a fellow of the David & Lucille Packard foundation.

ABOUT THE VERITAS FORUM

The Veritas Forum hosts university events that engage students and faculty in discussions about life's hardest questions and the relevance of Jesus Christ to all of life.

Every year, hundreds of university community members host, plan and coordinate a Veritas Forum on their local campuses, with guidance from national and regional staff across North America, Europe and Asia.

We seek to inspire the shapers of tomorrow's culture to connect their hardest questions with the person and story of Jesus Christ.

For more information about The Veritas Forum, including recordings and upcoming events, visit www.veritas.org.

Made in the USA
Charleston, SC
26 April 2014